Confronting
the
Enemies Within

The Journey Study Series

Confronting the Enemies Within

A Thomas Nelson Study Series
Based on *The Journey*
by
BILLY GRAHAM

THOMAS NELSON
Since 1798

NASHVILLE   DALLAS   MEXICO CITY   RIO DE JANEIRO   BEIJING

Published in Nashville, Tennessee. Thomas Nelson is a trademark of Thomas Nelson, Inc.

Thomas Nelson, Inc., titles may be purchased in bulk for educational, business, fund-raising, or sales promotional use. For information, please e-mail SpecialMarkets@ThomasNelson.com.

Unless otherwise noted, all Scripture quotations are taken from *The Holy Bible*, NEW INTERNATIONAL VERSION®. NIV®. Copyright © 1973, 1978, 1984 by International Bible Society. Used by permission of Zondervan. All rights reserved.

Confronting the Enemies Within: A Thomas Nelson Study Series Based on The Journey *by Billy Graham*

ISBN-13: 978-1-4185-1772-4
ISBN-10: 1-4185-1772-0

Printed in the United States of America

07 08 09 10 11 RRD 5 4 3 2 1

Contents

1

What
Went
Wrong?

To GET THE MOST FROM THIS STUDY GUIDE, READ
pages 32–38 of *The Journey*.

> *God is real—but so are evil and suffering, and we see*
> *them everywhere we look. But you need to remember:*
> *This is not the way God meant it to be.*
>
> BILLY GRAHAM
> *The Journey*

THINK ABOUT IT

If things go wrong, don't go with them.

—ROGER BABSON[1]

I do not understand what I do. . . . For what I do is not the
good I want to do; no, the evil I do not want to do—this I
keep on doing.

—ROMANS 7:15, 19

Raising children is full of life lessons. One of the most profound lessons happens when a child is asked, "Why did you do that?" The reply, "I don't know," is an honest and telling statement of the human condition. By nature, we are prone to do wrong. Therefore, if left unchecked, our natures will lead us into actions that are inconsistent with a thriving relationship with God.

Why is it this way? The world is not the way God intended it to be. All we have to do is look around and we see the evidence of sin—disease, destruction, perversion, and pain. There was a time when the world was perfect, without sin, and peaceful. But something happened in paradise, and things have never been the same.

REWIND

What are the biggest problems facing you and your family?

_____

_____

_____

_____

What is God's role in solving these problems?

_____

_____

_____

_____

People have long wondered why a loving God allows evil to exist. The Bible itself offers no complete explanation, but that doesn't seem to satisfy many curious souls. Therefore, people attempt to apply human rationale to godly actions, and the results are never clear-cut. Is God's plan for us to understand His reasoning?

Read 2 Thessalonians 2:7. How is evil characterized?

_____ A rational process

_____ An acceptable event

_____ A mystery

_____ Other: _____

What does this say about our ability to understand evil?

_____

_____

_____

_____

God and evil are both real. No amount of positive thinking will make evil disappear. No self-help book will make us immune to its effects. The headlines announce evil's power every day.

JOURNEY THROUGH GOD'S WORD

It bothers some people that God's ways often don't conform to human reasoning. This is the mystery that is woven throughout the entire revelation of God. The idea of "mystery" is best analyzed by studying the Book of Daniel. In this Old Testament book, a mystery is something that cannot be understood apart from God's revelation.

In the New Testament, Jesus referred to the mysteries of the kingdom of God. In Matthew 13:11, Jesus told His

---

disciples that He used parables because the people were unable to understand the deeper truths of God.

Paul used the term more than twenty times in reference to past revelations of God (see Ephesians 1:9; Colossians 2:2; and 1 Timothy 3:16). The book of Revelation contains four uses of the term in reference to various symbols.[2]

After years of attempting to explain God, many modern Bible scholars are willing to admit their inability to unravel His mysteries. Today's younger generation is seeking a God who still works in mysterious ways. They are completely comfortable with explaining something as just "a God thing."

We rob God of His uniqueness when we attempt to limit Him to human rationale. God doesn't think like us; He doesn't respond like us; He doesn't see things like us. Beware of anyone who offers explanations for God's mysteries because, in doing so, that person has claimed an awareness of the mind of God that humans are incapable of having.

Evil—we can't explain it, can't escape it, can't ignore it. So, what is its purpose in our lives? How did we get to this point? It's a familiar story that is worth another look.

RETHINK

What is "good," and how do you know if something is good or bad?

_____

_____

_____

To understand "good" we must return to the very first chapter of the first book of the Bible—Genesis—and the story of creation. A quick glance over the first chapter of Genesis reveals a constant refrain—God's creation was good. Throughout the unfolding of creation, God equated His perfection with "good." Therefore, God was and is the standard by which good is determined.

Think about your daily life and the things that you enjoy on a regular basis. Which of the following were parts of God's initial declaration of "good"?

_____ Television

_____ Humanity

_____ Celebrities

_____ Sports

_____ Hobbies

_____ Cell phones

_____ Computers

_____ Automobiles

_____ Homes

_____ Bank accounts

_____ Social organizations

_____ Fashion

We can conclude, therefore, that authentic goodness doesn't depend on the items in the list above. Real goodness exists in and through God alone. The "good life" has been wrongly defined as dependent on things that were not a part of God's initial definition of goodness.

What is the "good life" to you?

_____

_____

_____

Will the things you consider "good" lead you closer to or farther from God? Explain your response.

_____

_____

_____

_____

REFLECT

After the physical elements of the world were created, God crafted humanity. The environment was perfect; the people were perfect; life was good. The people were in a right relationship with God. They communed with Him. The Bible describes their relationship as being friendly.

Are you a friend of God? Why or why not?

_____

_____

_____

_____

Adam and Eve, however, were given free wills. Otherwise they would have been nothing more than robots. They had the opportunity to serve or to reject God. They had the choice to keep God's commands or to disobey God's commands. That choice is inherent in every human being.

You also have the capacity to obey or to disobey God. How do you know if you are being obedient or disobedient?

_____ What I'm doing feels good.

_____ What I'm doing draws attention to me.

_____ What I'm doing is in my best interest.

_____ What I'm doing is in line with the truth of God's Word.

How can you know the truth of God's Word?

_____ Attend church occasionally.

_____ Watch religious programming on television.

_____ Send my children to church.

_____ Invest time studying God's Word alone and in community with other believers.

Many believers want the benefit of an intimate relationship with God without investing the time in developing it. We have become a culture fixated on quick fixes and shortcuts. But with God, quick fixes and shortcuts often have tragic consequences.

Let's analyze the situation in which Adam and Eve lived and discover the mistakes they made that resulted in the condition in which we now live.

1. **They made a choice to love God** (Genesis 2:25). The relationship with God was a friendly one. They interacted with God without shame. God was the focus of their very existence.

Describe the time when you first chose to love God.

_____

_____

_____

_____

What, if anything, has changed since that time?

_____

_____

_____

_____

2. **They made a choice to reject God** (Genesis 3:1–6).
   The instructions regarding the tree in the middle of
   the garden were clear—stay away from it. Satan used
   the very thing God prohibited as a temptation to
   draw Adam and Eve away from God. Today, Satan
   uses the same tactics to interfere with our relationships with God.

What are the things Satan uses to distract you?

_____

_____

_____

_____

How do you feel when you give in to his deception?

_____

_____

_____

_____

Satan had been an angel, but he planned a coup in which he would take over God's place. As a result, he was expelled from heaven and his life work became anything that opposes God and His purposes.

Read Luke 10:18 and Isaiah 14:12–14. What do these two passages say about Satan?

_____

_____

_____

Satan's existence and the existence of evil are mysteries we cannot understand. God, being all-powerful, could have destroyed Satan rather than let him roam the earth. But that wasn't God's plan. Satan was allowed to exist as a force with which you and I must deal on a constant basis.

Read the following passages and list what each says about Satan.

Revelation 12:9–10

_____

_____

_____

John 8:44

_____

_____

_____

1 Thessalonians 3:5

_____

_____

_____

1 John 3:12

_____

_____

_____

1 Peter 5:8

_____

_____

_____

In what ways have you experienced Satan fulfilling these purposes in attempting to distract you from God's plans for your life?

_____

_____

_____

> *What a powerful temptation: to become like God! And in that terrible moment Adam and Eve turned their backs on God's truth and believed Satan's lie instead. They rebelled against the One who had made them, renouncing His friendship and choosing to go their own way. This is the essence of sin: rebellion against God.*
>
> BILLY GRAHAM
> *The Journey*

When we study Satan's strategy for distracting Adam and Eve, we discover a pattern that still is employed today—Satan called God's Word into question (Genesis 3:4–5). Satan told Adam and Eve that God was not being truthful with them. Satan not only lied, but he created a false rationale for the lie. Satan created distrust in the hearts of Adam and Eve. As a result, Adam and Eve chose their way instead of God's way.

What were the consequences of their actions? We often refer to it as "the Fall of Man." Adam and Eve fell into a way of life that still exists today. They disobeyed God and became acquainted with evil. They were kicked out of the Garden of Eden—paradise—and made to live with the consequences of their sin (Genesis 3:23–24).

Some refer to paradise as the perfect life. What are you doing to try to discover the perfect life?

_____

_____

_____

It might not seem fair that you and I have to suffer because of what Adam and Eve did back then. But sin's effects cannot be undone.

Read Genesis 3:14–19. What was the result of sin for each of the following?

The serpent

_____

_____

_____

The woman

_____

_____

_____

The man

_____

_____

_____

Notice that the consequence for the man was not work; the work was simply made more difficult. Man was created to work in the garden. As a result of sin, the ground was made uncooperative.

Read Romans 5:12. What was the universal effect of Adam and Eve's sin?

_____

_____

_____

The sin of Adam and Eve is repeated day after day in the life of every person on the planet. Some of us even want to take God's place because we believe we know what we need better than God does.

REACT

Sin affects your life and mine. We first are affected by our own sins, and then we sometimes are affected by the sins of other people. The Bible teaches that sin separates us from God because God can't be where sin is present. Think about what that means on a daily basis.

Describe a time when you felt distant from God.

_____

_____

_____

What do you think caused the distance?

_____

_____

_____

What is a situation you are facing right now in which you desperately need God?

_____

_____

_____

What can you do to make sure your relationship with God isn't hampered by your sin?

_____

_____

_____

_____

_____

_____

We can't honestly commit to not sinning. We can try not to sin, but sin is such a natural part of who we are that we can't eliminate it from our lives. We can, however, commit to having God's perspective on our sin and asking the Holy Spirit to convict us of sin so that our relationships with God are not weakened.

Since the fall of Adam and Eve, mankind has been searching for paradise. Today, what many people consider to be paradise is just a weak imitation of the real thing. What would it be like to live in a place where there is no sin and no disease, no evil and no jealousy? It would be heaven, because that is exactly what heaven is.

> *Try as we might, happiness and perfection elude us.*
> *The reason is because we too are fallen creatures, living*
> *in a fallen world. Adam and Eve's sin affected not only*
> *their lives, but ours as well. The consequences of their*
> *rebellion against God have come down to us.*
>
> BILLY GRAHAM
> *The Journey*

What are three truths you learned in this study, and how will you apply each truth to your daily life?

1. _____

   _____

   _____

   _____

2. _____

   _____

   _____

   _____

3. _____

_____

_____

_____

2

Sin's Devastation

T O GET THE MOST FROM THIS STUDY GUIDE, READ pages 38–42 of *The Journey*.

> *Never lose sight of the seriousness of sin. Its corruption has affected everything: our bodies, our minds, our emotions, our wills, our souls, our institutions, our world—everything.*
>
> BILLY GRAHAM
> *The Journey*

THINK ABOUT IT

Sin and the child of God are incompatible. They may occasionally meet; they cannot live together in harmony.

—JOHN R. W. STOTT[1]

For the wages of sin is death, but the gift of God is eternal life in Christ Jesus our Lord.

—ROMANS 6:23

We all have had moments when we have reflected on an event and realized it was more painful than we expected it to be. The desired consequences and the real consequences of our actions can differ considerably.

Sometimes we don't even consider the consequences of our actions; we simply do what we want to do, then hope for the best. That is a dangerous way to live because the consequences often are longer lasting than the situation that produced them.

Many people—even some Christians—don't see sin as anything to be concerned about. Our world is so comfortable with ungodliness that being godly is often less accepted than participating in sin. But sin does have consequences in your life, my life, and the lives of those all around us.

REWIND

What is your most common sin?

_____ Anger

_____ Lust

_____ Dishonesty

_____ Stealing

_____ Unfaithfulness

_____ Jealousy

_____ Idolatry

_____ Rebellion

_____ Other: _____

What are the spiritual effects of these sins?

_____

_____

_____

Sin is like a deadly disease—it is contagious and can be out of control before it is diagnosed. But, you do get paid to sin.

Read Romans 6:23. What is the pay due someone who sins?

_____

_____

_____

The death that accompanies sin is spiritual death. Like I said earlier, sin separates us from God. Eternity in hell is the only option for someone whose sin has not been forgiven. People don't go to hell because God is mean; they go to hell because He is just. Therefore, someone who dies without having asked Jesus Christ for forgiveness suffers the ultimate in sin's devastation—eternity separated from God in hell. But this is not God's will for us!

JOURNEY THROUGH GOD'S WORD

When we think about gardens in the Bible, we most often think about the Garden of Eden. It was planted by God (Genesis 2:8) and inhabited and tended by Adam and Eve. Following their sin, Adam and Eve were kicked out of the Garden of Eden and prevented from returning there. The precise location of the garden is unknown, but many speculate it to be in the area where the Tigris and Euphrates rivers meet in modern-day Iraq.

Gardens maintained their significance throughout the Bible. They often represented God's provision and blessing. Most gardens were surrounded by hedges or walls and were near the home of the owner. A garden required a substantial water source. Sometimes small orchards and vineyards were called gardens.

Gardens contained flowers, herbs, vegetables, fruit trees, and nut trees. Gardens were primarily a source of food for the owner, but they also had aesthetic value. Gardens were also places for solitude and prayer (Matthew 26:36–46).[2] A garden represented God's presence, and that's something we all need more of in our lives. The next time you are out enjoying nature, take a moment to quietly consider God's goodness and provision.

Once sin entered into the picture, it became a reality for all of humanity. Sin is costly and more devastating than most people imagine it to be. Let's consider the consequences of sin.

RETHINK

When do you consider the consequences of your sin?

_____ When I get caught

_____ Before I do it

_____ After I do it

_____ There are no consequences for sin.

When Adam and Eve sinned, there were both immediate and permanent consequences. Let's look at how their rebellion affected the entire world.

1. *Death entered the world.*
   God designed us to live forever in a perfect place with Him. But when Adam and Eve sinned, they received its wages—death.

Read Hebrews 9:27. What do you expect to happen at judgment?

_____

_____

_____

Death is inevitable. The real question is, "How prepared are you to face death and judgment?"

2. *We became separated from God.*
   When Adam and Eve sinned, they hid themselves from God (Genesis 3:8). Whereas they once were God's friends, they suddenly found themselves fearing Him.

What makes you afraid of God?

_____

_____

_____

Adam and Eve were overwhelmed with shame and guilt. As a result, their relationship with God was broken.

Read Isaiah 59:2. What has separated you from God?

_____

_____

_____

3. *We became alienated from each other.*

When questioned about their actions, Adam and Eve began to look for someone else to blame. Adam blamed Eve; Eve blamed the serpent. Then, once cast from the garden, Adam and Eve's sons were involved in a tragic story of a family relationship gone bad.

When you sin, who do you blame?

_____

_____

_____

4. *We became subject to God's judgment.*
   Sin is an offense to God, and we stand guilty before
   His perfect judgment. There is no rationale that will
   explain away our rebellious behavior.

**Read Psalm 7:11. What kind of judge is God? What does this
term mean to you?**

_____

_____

_____

5. *We became slaves of sin.*
   Adam and Eve were totally committed to their relationship with God until they were persuaded that
   they could be like God. Rather than live in a right
   relationship with God, they chose slavery to sin.

Have you ever sinned?

_____ Yes

_____ No

Read John 8:34. How does this verse interpret your answer to the question above?

_____

_____

_____

6. *The whole creation was corrupted.*

Can you imagine a world with no problems? That's what it was like in the Garden of Eden prior to the fall. But because of Adam and Eve's sin, everything changed.

Read Genesis 3:17–18. What was the result of Adam's sin?

_____

_____

_____

Read Romans 8:21. When will things return to the way God intended them?

_____

_____

_____

The fact is that we are affected by sin in every aspect of our existence. There is no way to escape sin's effects. People try to reverse the aging process, but to no avail. Our minds weaken with age, and we often suffer tragic and debilitating conditions. Our emotions, wills, and souls all are affected by sin. Not only that, but every human institution is affected by sin because it is operated by humans.

REFLECT

Do thoughts lead to actions or actions lead to thoughts? Scripture teaches that a person's thought life is more powerful than we might imagine. The things we think come out in the words we say and the deeds we do.

Have you ever been a part of . . .

_____ Slander?

_____ Lying?

_____ Cursing?

_____ Gossiping?

_____ Speaking unkindly?

Read James 3:6. What is the effect of your tongue in your life and in the lives of others?

_____

_____

_____

_____

_____

_____

_____

What about your mind? Are you thinking godly thoughts or are you falling into Satan's trap?

Consider each of the following characteristics. How prevalent are these characteristics in your thought life? Rank from 1 to 5, with 1 being "this isn't a problem" and 5 being "this is a constant struggle."

_____ Lust

_____ Hate

_____ Anger

_____ Bitterness

_____ Jealousy

_____ Greed

_____ Envy

_____ Selfishness

_____ Doubt

Total your score . . . if you scored more than 9, your mind is susceptible to being used as an agent of sin in your life.

The Ten Commandments were given to govern how God's people interacted with God and each other. Some of the commandments govern interpersonal behavior, and others govern the relationship with God. The bottom line is that we sin whenever we live in any way that is inconsistent with God's Word.

Which of your thoughts or actions does God not know?

_____

_____

_____

_____

Read Proverbs 20:27. What does God know about you?

_____

_____

_____

_____

We've considered things that we do that fall into the category of sin. However, you also can sin by not doing something you should do.

What is something you know God wants you to do that you are not doing?

Real peace in life cannot be found until you stop doing the things God says not to do and start doing the things God says to do. If you struggle with obedience in either area, you will struggle in your spiritual life.

Our inner soul is infected with sin. As a result of its presence in our lives, we commit sins—specific actions that we know are wrong based on our understanding of God's Word. The indwelling power of the Holy Spirit is the only thing we have that can wage war against sin. Otherwise, we are destined to struggle personally and spiritually.

Through self-discipline we might get rid of some of our sins, but our basic problem of sin remains untouched and untouchable, lurking just beneath the surface and ready to strike at any moment. Don't ever think sin is only a minor misdeed or an occasional outburst of wrongdoing. Sin is far deeper than that. It is a spiritual disease that leaves us weak and powerless. Its hold over us is so strong that only God can overcome it.

BILLY GRAHAM
The Journey

What are some things you can do to improve your awareness of the sins you commit?

_____

_____

_____

_____

_____

What should you do if you come to the realization one day that you no longer sin?

_____

_____

_____

_____

REACT

Sin is the universal problem of the human race. It is a spiritual disease that leaves us weak and powerless. It has a grip on us that only God can break. People try all sorts of things hoping to make their lives better, but they are unsuccessful.

What are some things you have done to try to make your life better?

_____

_____

_____

_____

On a scale of 1 to 5, with 5 being total success, how successful have you been at improving your life apart from focusing on your relationship with God? Explain your response.

_____

_____

_____

Sin lives inside each of us and works to distract us from doing the things that God would have us do. Sin can be an inappropriate focus on something good—we can spend too much time on a hobby and too little time studying God's Word. Some of the most dangerous sins are those things that, in and of themselves, are good things. They become sin when we give them attention that is due to God and His purposes.

We can even sin while doing something for God—if our reasons for doing it are other than to glorify God. Some people enter into ministry so that they can be popular. Some people lead a small-group study to stroke their own egos. Some people get involved in prayer ministry so they can know what's happening in the lives of other people.

We shouldn't be skeptical of everyone who is serving God; but we must be mindful of our own motives for serving God. If you desire to glorify God, then serve Him. But if your desire is anything else, your service to God is sin in your life.

What are some areas of ministry in which God might use you?

_____

_____

_____

_____

What can you do to guard against entering into these ministries for the wrong purposes?

_____

_____

_____

_____

You can do the right thing for the right reason; the right thing for the wrong reason; the wrong thing for the right reason; and the wrong thing for the wrong reason.

In the space below, list an example of a time when you have done each of these things.

The right thing for the right reason

_____

_____

_____

The right thing for the wrong reason

_____

_____

_____

The wrong thing for the right reason

_____

_____

_____

The wrong thing for the wrong reason

_____

_____

_____

Which of the above is the most subtle to you? Why?

_____

_____

_____

What should you do to guard against this weakness?

_____

_____

_____

> *Remember: This world is not the way God meant it to be, and neither are we. Something devastating has happened—and that "something" is sin. But life can be different. We don't need to be crippled any longer by the disease of sin—because God has provided the cure.*
>
> BILLY GRAHAM
> *The Journey*

What are three truths you learned in this study, and how will you apply each truth to your daily life?

1. _____

   _____

   _____

   _____

   _____

2. _____

_____

_____

_____

_____

3. _____

_____

_____

_____

_____

3

Prone
to
Wander

T O GET THE MOST FROM THIS STUDY GUIDE, READ pages 155–160 of *The Journey.*

> *If God is for us, why do we have so many problems? Christians aren't exempt from them; we too experience illness, temptation, disappointment, grief, and a hundred other problems we could list. Our journey through life is filled with all kinds of hazards and bumps in the road, and will be until we enter heaven.*
>
> BILLY GRAHAM
> *The Journey*

THINK ABOUT IT

The basic problem most people have is that they're doing nothing to solve their basic problem.

—BOB RICHARDSON[1]

Watch and pray so that you will not fall into temptation.
The spirit is willing, but the body is weak.

—MATTHEW 26:41

Problems are everywhere; we can't seem to escape them. Some people say that the older we get, the more problems we have. However, it could be that the older we get, the more aware we are of the problems.

What constitutes a problem? The dictionary defines a *problem* as "a situation, matter, or person that presents perplexity or difficulty." Therefore, a problem can be something over which you and I can exercise no control, or it can be something inside of us that we just can't seem to master.

Problems often lead to stress, and stress often derails our capacity to reason and make faith-based decisions. Maybe you've seen someone you know who is spiritually strong make a decision that baffles you. It might be that the stress associated with a specific problem contributed to the inexplicable action.

REWIND

What are your most common sources of stress?

____ Children

____ Work

____ Finances

_____ Social pressures

_____ Relationships

_____ Habits

_____ Personal desires

_____ Health

_____ Other: _____

What happens to you when you experience these stresses?

_____ I turn to God.

_____ I try to fight them but am unsuccessful.

_____ I ignore them.

_____ I give in and hope for the best.

The world doesn't offer us much help; it seems to be working to distract us from God's plans and purposes. If that's your perception, then you are right. We are vulnerable to life's stresses and temptations because of what happens around us. Today, we are more aware of what happens around us than ever before. We not only know what happens in our homes, but we can also tune in and learn what happened around the world while we slept. Some people give in to temptation because they perceive that everyone is doing the very thing they are trying to resist.

We aren't much help either. Another reason that we are vulnerable to life's stresses and temptations is our own inner weaknesses. We lack a solid "what if" plan for dealing with pressures that we know are coming.

JOURNEY THROUGH GOD'S WORD

What is temptation? In general, it is anything that entices us to do or think something that is inconsistent with God's character. We see early in the Bible that the ultimate source of temptation in the lives of believers is Satan. Adam, Eve, Abraham, and David succumbed to the temptation. Job and Jesus faced temptation and held their ground.

The first thing to remember about temptation is that God is not the source of temptation (James 1:13). All temptation, however, passes through God's permissive filter. Why would God allow temptation in the life of His child? Believers often face testing to produce patience and faith in order to honor God and bring glory to Him. James 1:12 tells us that those who endure temptation without giving in will be blessed.

How does temptation happen? James explains that the initial source of temptation is an individual's evil desires (James 1:14). That was the source of Adam and Eve's temptation—they wanted to be like God. They desired something that God did not desire for them. We often can trace our temptations to the very same source.

It isn't God's plan for us to give in to temptation. In Romans 12:21, Paul said that it is God's desire for us to overcome evil with good. However, if we do not resist the temptation in God's power, the temptation will lead to sin. Being tempted is not a sin; giving in to temptation is sin. In Matthew 5:28, Jesus further defined *sin* as desiring to do something in response to a temptation.

The good news is that God does not leave us powerless against temptation. In 1 Corinthians 10:13, Paul told the Christians in Corinth that (a) any temptation we face is common to all people; (b) God empowers believers to overcome the temptations they face; and (c) God will provide a way of escape.[2] There are two things to keep in mind regarding temptation—it is not God's desire for us to put ourselves in tempting situations, and our best response in some situations is fleeing the temptation rather than trying to fight it. Face it with God's power when necessary; run from it when possible. This is the recipe for dealing with temptation.

Maybe you've seen the cartoon characters where Satan sits on one shoulder and an angel sits on the other, whispering contradictory suggestions into the ears of a person. We laugh at this comic representation of temptation, but it is more accurate than we might believe. The main difference is that temptation is no laughing matter.

RETHINK

When you face temptation, what Scriptures come to mind?

Don't feel badly if you couldn't answer the question above. It serves to point out that many believers don't rely on one of their best defenses against temptation—God's Word. When temptation comes, it isn't always possible to get a copy of the Bible and begin searching for Scriptures to help you withstand the temptation. We must rely on the Scriptures we have committed to memory, and then trust the Holy Spirit to help us remember them.

Read Romans 8:26. What is the role of the Holy Spirit in our dealing with temptation?

_____

_____

_____

There is really no need to debate the reasons we experience temptation; the real issue is what we will do when we are tempted.

How are you prepared for each of the following situations?

a. A flat tire?

_____

b. A financial problem?

_____

c. A child's misbehavior?

_____

d. Temptation?

_____

The truth is that many of us spend more time preparing for the first three situations listed above and think little about the fourth item on the list. We don't consider a contingency plan for facing temptation. By the end of this lesson, that should change.

REFLECT

Temptation is being urged or enticed to do something wrong. This enticement comes from almost every area of life.

Which of the following can be sources of temptation for you?

_____ People

_____ Entertainment: television, music, movies

_____ Magazines

_____ The Internet

_____ Personal desires

_____ Ego

_____ Ambition

_____ Money and possessions

_____ Other: _____

Maybe you checked more items on the list than you imagined you would. The reality is that temptation comes from more places than we realize.

Read Matthew 4:4, 7, 10. What is the common phrase in these three verses?

_____

_____

_____

Jesus had a predetermined strategy for dealing with temptation. He didn't wait until He was in the midst of the temptation to begin looking for ways to escape it. Jesus knew God's Word and relied on it to drive Satan away. His strategy serves as a great model for us. Many Christians don't realize they are being tempted until they are in the middle of the experience. By that point, they might find escape difficult, if not impossible.

Satan wanted to distract Jesus and prevent Him from carrying out His redemptive mission on earth. Satan also wants to distract you and keep you from fulfilling your purpose on earth. We have seen countless spiritual leaders fall victim to temptation and forfeit their ministries. Satan rejoices when a believer is debilitated by the sin that results from temptation.

Read 1 Peter 5:8. What is the ultimate source of all temptation?

_____

_____

_____

According to the verse above, what is Satan's purpose?

_____

_____

_____

Read 2 Corinthians 11:14. How does Satan conduct his business?

_____

_____

_____

Satan works in two ways to tempt us. In order to be properly prepared to defend ourselves against temptation, we must know how he works.

1. **Satan pressures us from the outside.**

   The world around us is a constant source of temptation. The world's way of thinking is the real threat to the spiritual health of believers.

> *Never forget: We live in an upside-down world, in which people hate what they should love and love what they should hate. This inner attitude puts self at the center of life instead of God. Its outlook is limited to the present, and its values come from our pride and selfish desires.*
>
> BILLY GRAHAM
> *The Journey*

What are some common beliefs that are contrary to God's standards?

_____

_____

_____

How do you respond when you face people who hold to these beliefs?

_____

_____

_____

Read 1 John 2:15–17. List in the space below the specific "ways of the world" referenced in this passage.

_____

_____

_____

Are these pressures real in your life?

_____ Yes

_____ No

We must be on guard against worldliness in our lives. Even in interactions among believers, worldly attitudes can creep in. Personal disputes and hard feelings are signs of spiritual immaturity (1 Corinthians 3:3).

2. Satan pressures us from within ourselves.
   The Bible refers to "the flesh" as symbolic of a deter-
   mination to satisfy our personal desires and appetites
   to the exclusion of pleasing God.

Read Romans 8:5. Substitute the definition of "flesh" above
into this verse and rewrite it in the space below.

_____

_____

_____

Are you living your life to satisfy your own desires and
appetites? _____ How can you keep this from being your
desire?

_____

_____

_____

The Bible challenges us to rule over our bodies, not to be ruled
by them. Yet people often give in to their physical desires in

the form of lust, alcohol or drug abuse, overeating, failing to exercise, and so forth. James 1:14 warns that these desires have the ability to drag us away from God's purposes for our lives. We also can be dragged away by things that aren't as self-destructive as the things listed above. A person can place so much emphasis on something good—such as work—that he or she neglects God's plans. This is also an example of giving in to temptation.

REACT

What is the antidote to temptation? Some people don't believe temptation can be defeated. Yet Scripture gives us a one-step solution.

Read Romans 12:1. What should be your offering to God?

If you were raised in the church, you are probably familiar with offering envelopes in which people often place their tithe before giving it to the church. The offering envelope serves to identify the source of the offering and the purposes for which it is given. Think about each day being an offering envelope, and see yourself being placed into that envelope and laid at the foot of God's throne. You are, in effect, saying, "God, I am giving myself to You for Your purposes." Each day should include that mental activity. Doing so reinforces the truth of Romans 12:1 in your life and serves to help defend you against temptation.

Before leaving the house each morning, we consider how we should be dressed. This is a difficult decision for some people. It is governed by the weather, the activity, and current fashion.

Read Romans 13:14. How should you be dressed before beginning each day?

_____

_____

_____

Committing ourselves to God for His purposes must be a continual process lest we become complacent and fall victim to Satan's schemes. Are you prepared for the temptations that will come?

Today's society encourages people to be infatuated with their bodies. We have lost the sense of appropriateness and modesty that was once characteristic of a more God-fearing culture. Some Christians even dress in ways that become temptations and stumbling blocks to other believers.

Are you being a distraction to others in the way that you dress?

_____ Yes

_____ No

_____ I honestly haven't thought about it.

Your response might be, "Well, if people are distracted by me, that's their problem. It's not my intent to be a temptation." That's a nice thought, but it reflects an attitude that is contrary to Scripture.

Read 1 Corinthians 10:32. What is the instruction regarding causing someone else to stumble?

_____

_____

_____

God gave us our bodies, and we are to take care of them and use them for His glory. But all too often we allow our bodies to rule us, instead of us ruling them. Have you committed your body to Christ?

BILLY GRAHAM
The Journey

What are three truths you learned in this study, and how will
you apply each truth to your daily life?

1. _____

_____

_____

_____

2. _____

_____

_____

_____

3. _____

_____

_____

_____

4

The Way of Escape

T O GET THE MOST FROM THIS STUDY GUIDE, READ
pages 160–164 of *The Journey.*

The real question is this: How should we deal with
temptation? How can we resist it? Don't forget: temp-
tation means being tempted to do wrong in the eyes of
God. Label sin for what it is: sin.

BILLY GRAHAM
The Journey

THINK ABOUT IT

When you flee temptation, don't leave a forwarding address.
—ANONYMOUS[1]

Do not conform any longer to the pattern of this world,
but be transformed by the renewing of your mind.

—ROMANS 12:2

Temptation comes at our weakest points. Satan has no intention to force open locked doors to the safe; he simply sneaks in through the small cracks we leave in less secure doors. Satan wants to tempt us at our most vulnerable places.

Because we have fallen victim to temptation so many times before, we can begin to believe that resisting it is impossible. It becomes easier to ask forgiveness than to put up a fight. We are given the privilege of God's forgiveness, but forgiveness doesn't erase sin's consequences. Wouldn't it be more effective in our spiritual lives to resist the temptation, avoid the sin, and eliminate the consequences?

REWIND

When you realize you have sinned, what do you do?

_____

_____

_____

Think about the last time you gave in to a temptation. What might be an effective strategy for defeating that temptation the next time you face it?

_____

_____

_____

The story is a familiar one. The Israelites were camped on one hill, the Philistines on a hill on the other side of the valley. The Israelites knew they had God on their side, but the Philistines were big . . . very big! Goliath, the champion warrior of the Philistines, seemed to enjoy screaming his threats across the valley at the terrified nation that had seen God do incredible things on their behalf. Their leader, Saul, was spiritually weak and, therefore, he didn't know how to appropriate God's power.

Into the camp came David. He was on a mission from his father to deliver food to his brothers, who were soldiers. David saw what was going on and understood something the king failed to realize—the battle wasn't between the Philistines and the Israelites, but between evil and God. The outcome of the battle, therefore, already was determined. David wasn't afraid. He went up against the giant with a slingshot and some stones. You know the rest of the story.

The Philistines weren't defeated by a small boy and a well-placed rock; they were defeated by God's power. David could have won the battle with a twig because the real battle was God's. David simply knew how to let God fight the battle in and through him.

JOURNEY THROUGH GOD'S WORD

When the nation of Israel prepared to leave Egypt, we get a glimpse of a potential problem that the Israelites would face over and over. In Exodus 13:17, the Bible says that God did not lead the Israelites toward Philistia because they might return to Egypt when they faced the warriors who inhabited the land. The path through Philistia was the shortest route from Egypt to Canaan, but the Philistines stood in the way.

The Philistines would continue to be a threat to the Israelites. During the time of the judges, the Philistines were the most significant threat to the nation of Israel. They are mentioned in the story of Samson (Judges 13–16) and eventually invaded portions of the Israelite territory. The Philistines captured the Ark of the Covenant only to try to dispose of it because of its power.

The Philistine threat intensified until the battle between David and Goliath. With their champion slain, the

---

Philistines retreated, leaving their camp to the Israelites. Though they retreated, they did not disappear. Later, David actually sought refuge among the Philistines while he was running from Saul.

The Philistines were well-equipped and skilled. The nation had a good road system, horses, chariots, and metal weapons. David selected men from among the Philistines to be his palace guards in Jerusalem.[2] Though the Philistines were real, they represent the antagonizing power of temptation in the life of someone seeking to serve God. At first, God diverted the Israelites away from the Philistines. Perhaps God intended for the wilderness experience and conquest of the Promised Land to serve as times of spiritual growth for His people. However, the nation was no better prepared for an encounter with the Philistines.

We are that way when it comes to temptation. God gives us a way around temptation and offers us opportunities to be strengthened spiritually so we can withstand the temptation. Yet we often fail to heed God's educational offerings so we face temptation with our own power and are afraid. The secret to spiritual victory is spiritual preparation.

The key to defeating temptation isn't found in your own power; it's found in the power of the God we serve. But how do we make use of that power?

RETHINK

In the event of an emergency in your home, what is your plan of escape?

_____

_____

_____

_____

_____

You probably have some alternate paths to work, school, church, and even the grocery store. You may remember being in school and participating in fire or tornado drills. In some places, there are earthquake or hurricane drills. Along the coast and in snowy areas are evacuation routes that are intended to be the safest passage from the area in the event of a natural disaster. We go to great extremes to be prepared for the physical dangers we might face.

Do you need a spiritual evacuation route? Why or why not?

_____

_____

_____

_____

Have you ever made a resolution and failed to keep it? A resolution is a promise to change something that needs to be changed. But many people fail to keep their resolutions because they lack personal power over the situation or the issue. We can't make a resolution to resist temptation because we lack the power to enforce the resolution. You and I do not have the power to resist Satan's attacks, but there is Someone who has that power. Do you know Him?

REFLECT

There are four steps that are necessary if you are going to escape temptation and the sin it produces.

1. **Recognize temptation.**

   Temptation is easy to recognize . . . after the fact. It's easy to look back and see what went wrong. But how can we recognize temptation in advance? Your ability to recognize temptation is dependent upon your knowledge of God's standards of right and wrong. This is where many people come up short because they have accepted the world's belief that there is no universal standard of right and wrong.

How do you determine right from wrong?

_____ There is no standard of right and wrong.

_____ Right is anything that makes me happy.

_____ Right is whatever seems right at the moment.

_____ Right is what God says is right.

Why is it so hard to know right from wrong?

_____ Because the standard is ambiguous.

_____ Because I don't know the standard—God's Word.

_____ Because the Bible says one thing and the world says something else.

_____ Because I choose to ignore the standard.

You will recognize temptation when you ask God to help you recognize it. This includes both the obvious and the subtle temptations. Make Psalm 139:23 your prayer. Ask God to search you and to point out your weaknesses so you will be less vulnerable in those areas.

But what about those areas that the Bible doesn't address? What should we do when we are forced to make a decision without specific biblical counsel?

Ask yourself these questions:

- Does this glorify God?

- Can I thank God for this?

- Will this draw me closer to God?

- Will this help me spiritually or physically?

- Will this cause someone else to stumble spiritually or morally?

When in doubt, don't do it!

2. **When temptation comes, reject it.**
   Don't spend too much time with temptation. The more time you spend with it, the more comfortable you'll become.

> *Don't savor temptations; don't dwell on them or toy with them or replay them over and over in your mind. The more you think about a particular temptation, the more enticing it becomes. If you don't look out, it will become almost impossible to pull away.*
>
> BILLY GRAHAM
> *The Journey*

If someone placed a vial of deadly poison in your hand, what would you do?

_____ Take a sip

_____ Keep it around for fun

_____ Get as far away from it as possible

Temptation is like poison. It is dangerous, and we have no business being around it.

What is the advice related to sin in each of the following Scriptures?

2 Timothy 2:22

_____

_____

_____

1 Corinthians 10:14

_____

_____

_____

1 Corinthians 6:18

_____

_____

_____

When you are faced with temptation, take action. Turn off the television or the computer, get rid of the book or magazine, tactfully end the relationship, change jobs. Find another Christian with whom you can be accountable. Commit 1 Corinthians 10:13 to memory. Ask God to show you that way of escape and then run!

3. **Learn from your encounters with temptation.**
Our past experiences with temptation offer some valuable life lessons. By analyzing our past experiences, we can discover what works and doesn't work in response to temptation.

Who are the people that are sources of temptation to you?

_____

_____

_____

What are situations in which you most often are tempted?

_____

_____

_____

Which of your weaknesses are being exploited by Satan?

_____

_____

_____

_____

The source of many of our failures is pride. We make the mistake of placing too much stock in ourselves. Temptation can serve to reveal to us our areas of weakness and teach us how to be better prepared to face temptations in the future.

Avoid situations in which you will be vulnerable. If there is a person with whom you are particularly vulnerable, avoid being alone with that person. If there is a habit that is a problem, then have someone help keep you accountable.

4. **When you fail, repent and seek God's forgiveness.** Repentance and forgiveness always come in tandem. Without repentance, there is no forgiveness. Without the possibility of forgiveness, there is no repentance.

What happens to your relationship with God when you sin?

_____

_____

_____

What is the promise of 1 John 1:9?

_____

_____

_____

When we sin, we damage our relationship with God, but the relationship is not ended. God is disappointed in us, but He still loves us and wants to be in a right relationship with us.

REACT

The only sin God can't forgive is the sin of refusing His forgiveness. God still expects His people to be in right relationships with Him. That means He requires us to be free from sin and its effects. But He knows we can never be perfect.

That is why God sent His Son, Jesus Christ, to take our places. Jesus was the perfect sacrifice. When God looks at His children, He doesn't see them; He sees His Son. Without the sacrifice of His Son, we would be lost and without hope.

What gives you hope in life?

_____

_____

_____

How does your daily activity reveal this hope to people who have no hope?

_____

_____

_____

Satan wants you to believe you can't be forgiven. This is a lie. Even when you commit a sin and suffer significant consequences for your actions, forgiveness is available. God never gives up on you and never releases you from His grasp. You are His child. He loves you. He sent His Son to die for you. He wants to help you stand up under the pressures of living in a fallen world. Will you give God the honor of directing your life?

Every time the Israelites put away the Philistines, they breathed a sigh of relief. But their relief was short-lived. The Philistines found a way to become a problem time and time again. The Israelites were susceptible to the Philistines. The Philistines knew it; the Israelites knew it; God knew it.

The temptations that come at your most vulnerable points will not be easily defeated. The distraction will continue to be an issue so you will have to keep giving the issue to God. If you don't, you will find yourself growing more and more comfortable with it, and the issue will become more and more dangerous.

> *When you sin, don't excuse it or ignore it or blame it on someone else. Admit it . . . repent of it . . . and then rejoice that God has fully forgiven you.*
>
> BILLY GRAHAM
> *The Journey*

What are three truths you learned in this study, and how will you apply each truth to your daily life?

1. _____

_____

_____

_____

2. _____

   _____

   _____

   _____

3. _____

   _____

   _____

   _____

5

Why Did It Happen?

T O GET THE MOST FROM THIS STUDY GUIDE, READ pages 165–168 of *The Journey*.

> *God not only wants to change our actions; He also wants to change our hearts. In other words, God wants to change us both on the outside and the inside.*
>
> BILLY GRAHAM
> *The Journey*

THINK ABOUT IT

Beware of no man more than of yourself; we carry our worst enemies within us.

—CHARLES H. SPURGEON[1]

Create in me a pure heart, O God,
*   and renew a steadfast spirit within me.*

—PSALM 51:10

Our behaviors are rooted in our thoughts. It is possible, however, to fake it for a while. Maybe you've been on a movie set where skilled craftsmen have created a facade that fools the audience into believing the scene was actually filmed on location. It appears authentic, but it is a thin veil.

The same thing can happen in our spiritual lives. We can hide behind a facade of religious behavior without ever having experienced the internal heart change that should be the motivation for behavioral change. Then, when life turns upside down, our faith isn't able to sustain us. We crumble or back out on our commitments to Christ and choose to live with recklessness, leaving many to wonder if we really knew Jesus Christ at all.

REWIND

Place an X on the line indicating your spiritual strength.

Weak————————————————————Strong

Maybe you can relate to the story on page 165 of *The Journey*. An apparent spiritual giant abandoned her faith when advised that her life was nearing its end. Maybe she lived with the idea that her faith was more limiting than empowering. Perhaps she thought more about what she didn't get to do rather than the freedom that accompanies authentic faith. Either way, her relationship with God and her understanding of her faith were flawed.

There probably are a lot of people who share the problems this woman had—not her physical problems, but her spiritual problems. Too many people see their faith as nothing more than insurance against hell. But there's so much more than that.

JOURNEY THROUGH GOD'S WORD

In the Bible, the word *heart* is used as more than just a reference to one's blood-pumping organ. It is the very center of the physical aspect of life. The heart is made stronger through eating and drinking (Genesis 18:5), indicating that a healthy heart is something to be desired.

The heart also represents the entire person—both physical and spiritual. The heart is tied to a person's intellectual capacity, from which one reasons and makes decisions (Matthew 13:15). A person's thinking is rooted in his or her heart (Proverbs 23:7), and the heart is the place where we meditate on things (Psalm 139:23).

Worry also is connected to the heart. In the Bible, when people set their hearts on something, they usually gave it extra attention.

A person's actions are also connected to the heart. People think in their hearts and reason in their hearts. In Romans 1:24, the cravings of the heart are seen as something to be resisted.

In addition to the mind and the will, the heart is associated with feelings and affections. Joy begins in the heart (Psalm 4:7), despair is the heaviness of the heart (Proverbs 12:25), and sorrow is a troubled heart (Proverbs 25:20).

Love and hate are products of the heart, as is jealousy (James 3:14). Believers are challenged to love God with their hearts (Mark 12:30), and Paul said that authentic love is the product of a pure heart (1 Timothy 1:5).

The *heart* in Scripture represents the conscience, from which moral decisions are made. It also is used to describe the real character of a person. In 1 Samuel 16:7, we are told that man looks on the outward appearance, but God looks on the heart.

But not everything that comes from the heart is good. The Bible points out that depravity is rooted in the heart (Jeremiah 17:9). Jesus said that all sorts of negative thoughts and actions come from the heart (Matthew 15:8–11).

Because the heart is the source of so much evil, real transformation requires a change of heart. When God moves in, His Law is written on our hearts (Romans 2:15). When Saul was about to become king, God gave him a new heart (1 Samuel 10:9).

The heart is the place in which the Holy Spirit lives in a believer. Only as God gets control of our hearts can we truly be conformed to His image.[2]

There have been great advances in the area of cardiac health. Today, doctors can detect the warning signs and prescribe treatment to prevent heart attacks and stroke. But, with all of the effort to ensure cardiac health, have we forgotten the importance of spiritual health?

RETHINK

If God produced a picture of the spiritual health of your heart, what would it reveal?

____ My spiritual heart is perfectly healthy.

____ My spiritual heart has some signs of weakness.

____ My spiritual heart is in bad shape.

____ My spiritual heart needs to be renewed.

God wants to change the way you act, but He wants to change it from the inside out. God wants to affect the way you look at every area of life. He wants to change how you view your job, your family, and your money. He wants to give you a "heart transplant" in which your ways of thinking and acting are replaced by His ways of thinking and acting.

Is a change of heart possible in your life? Why or why not?

_____

_____

_____

We can't become the people God wants us to be by remaining the people we used to be. If nothing has changed, then we will not change. You can't have an encounter with God and be left the way you were. When God moves in, He begins a work in you that cannot be accomplished any other way.

REFLECT

> *Why is God so concerned with what goes on inside of us? The reason is simple: This is God's will. God's will is for us to become more and more like Christ. When we allow sinful thoughts and emotions to govern us, however, we fall far short of His plan. Christ was pure both within and without—and that must be our goal as well.*
>
> BILLY GRAHAM
> *The Journey*

Why does it matter what we think as long as we do the right thing?

_____

_____

_____

_____

God is concerned about what goes on inside of us. There is a difference between living by the rules and living by principles. Rules easily can be circumvented; principles are transferable.

What is God's will for your life? Read these verses and discover what each one says.

1 Thessalonians 4:3

_____

_____

_____

_____

2 Corinthians 7:1

_____

_____

_____

Matthew 23:27

_____

_____

_____

Matthew 23:27 was directed at religious people—those who looked the part but had not experienced a change of heart. Jesus wanted them to know that their inner hearts were important to God. Why are our inner hearts so important?

1. **Our thoughts determine our actions.**
   Our actions always reflect our inner thoughts. Even when you say something you didn't mean to say, it came from your inner thoughts. Even when you do

something you didn't mean to do, it happened as a response to your inner feelings and thoughts.

Read Matthew 15:19. What is inside our hearts?

_____

_____

_____

2. **God loves us and knows how destructive wrong thoughts and emotions can be.**

   Have you ever been the victim of someone's emotional breakdown? Have you ever had an emotional breakdown yourself? If so, you know how damaging they are. Few things said in an emotional outburst are uplifting.

Our minds and bodies are closely connected. Negative emotions have physical side effects. You probably are aware of a personal situation in which your emotions produced physical problems. From heart attacks to high blood pressure to rashes, emotions can affect our health.

Read Psalm 32:3–4. What happened to David when he tried to keep to himself the sin he committed with Bathsheba?

_____

_____

_____

Read Proverbs 17:22. What is the effect of a cheerful spirit?

_____

_____

_____

What is the effect of a crushed spirit?

_____

_____

_____

Which one would you rather have? Why?

_____

_____

_____

_____

David had to realize that his health was suffering because he had not dealt with his sin. Keeping it to himself was more dangerous than confessing it and seeking forgiveness. Though David's sin was against God, he paid a physical price for it.

Has there ever been a time when you suffered physically because of unconfessed sin in your life? How do you know the suffering was due to the sin?

_____

_____

_____

_____

We must be careful not to assign every ailment a sin-related cause. Some ailments are the result of sin, but some ailments are simply ailments. When it comes to telling the difference, sin-caused ailments are usually preceded by an extended period of time thinking about the situation. If you did something wrong and you've been thinking about it for a while, there is a good possibility that you will experience a physical ailment because of your concern.

If you are a believer, your conscience will help you determine if something is right or wrong. God won't leave you wondering. You won't have to experience a physical ailment and then try to backtrack and figure out just what you did wrong.

Sin has invaded every area of life—our bodies, our minds, and our wills. By nature, we are strangers to God with no hope for a peaceful future. But Jesus came to fix that problem.

Read Colossians 1:21–22. What was your past condition?

_____

_____

_____

_____

What is your condition when you accept Jesus Christ as Lord and Savior?

_____

_____

_____

REACT

Have you ever wanted to be holy and without fault before God? This might be the first time you've ever thought about it. People try all kinds of things in an effort to be perfect. People use cosmetic surgery to obtain physical perfection. Some parents desire genetic engineering to create perfect children. Some students obsess over making perfect grades. But all of these attempts are inadequate. The surgically altered person still is progressing toward death. Genetic engineering denies the fact that it is God who forms us in our mothers' wombs. Educational perfection is relative to the class and fellow students in the class. What was perfect work in one class might be average in another class. Perfection, though sought after, is elusive.

Some people desire the perfect life, perfect spouse, perfect home, perfect car, or perfect child. Others want the perfect job, perfect neighbor, perfect church, or perfect meal. Perfection is a standard that people can't seem to agree on.

What are some things you can do to be perfect?

_____

_____

_____

What are some things you can do to be perfect before God?

_____

_____

_____

We learned earlier that God is a righteous Judge. He has no choice but to deal with us in ways that are consistent with His character. Therefore, sin cannot go unpunished. You have several choices if you want to be right before God.

First, you can try to be good—perfect. You might try living without making any mistakes. You must be totally honest in every situation, think the right thoughts all the time, say the right thing in every situation. In other words, you can make no mistakes.

Is it possible for you to live the life described above? Why or why not?

_____

_____

_____

Your other option is to let the perfection of Jesus Christ overshadow your imperfection. This means you must accept what God says about you as being the truth, admit that you are powerless to fix the problem, and ask Him to come into your life and renew your heart.

Have you ever accepted Jesus' perfection as a substitute for yours? Explain how and when.

_____

_____

_____

This doesn't mean that we become perfect. It simply means that Jesus' perfection is what God sees when He looks at us. He doesn't see our tempers or our bad thoughts; He sees Jesus Christ and His sacrifice.

Our actions are always a reflection of our inner thoughts. In fact, sometimes it's almost impossible to separate our thoughts from our actions. This is why we need to submit our lives to Christ every day, for only He can transform our hearts and minds.

BILLY GRAHAM
The Journey

What are three truths you learned in this study, and how will you apply each truth to your daily life?

1. _____

_____

_____

_____

2. _____

_____

_____

_____

3. _____

_____

_____

_____

6

The
Enemies
Within

T O GET THE MOST FROM THIS STUDY GUIDE, READ pages 169–174 of *The Journey*.

What does God see when He looks within your heart and mind? You may hide your innermost thoughts from others, but you cannot hide them from God.

BILLY GRAHAM
The Journey

THINK ABOUT IT

One reason that sin flourishes is that it is treated like a cream puff instead of a rattlesnake.

—BILLY SUNDAY[1]

There are six things the LORD hates,
seven that are detestable to him:
haughty eyes,
a lying tongue,
hands that shed innocent blood,
a heart that devises wicked schemes,
feet that are quick to rush into evil,
a false witness who pours out lies
and a man who stirs up dissension among brothers.

—PROVERBS 6:16–19

We live in a self-absorbed world in which people spend a lot of time and effort in self-edification. Personal coaches can work on everything from one's wardrobe to one's job. Celebrities have people to manage their images, and politicians have spokespeople who communicate for them. Image management is a hot topic.

How often do we stop to think about God's perception of us? Some people believe God's truth can be renegotiated and redefined so that it fits into our lifestyles. There are even some churches that refuse to identify some social trends as sin. They have compromised what it means to be a believer and follower of Christ.

The most serious threats to our spiritual health aren't those that attack from the outside; they are the ones that come at us from the inside. In reality, we are our own worst enemies.

REWIND

On a scale of 1–5, with 1 being "this is not a problem" and 5 being "this is a serious problem," rank yourself in each of the following areas:

_____ Pride

_____ Anger

_____ Envy

_____ Impurity

_____ Gluttony

_____ Slothfulness

_____ Greed

The sins listed above have been referred to as the seven deadly sins. This list does not appear in this order in Scripture, but each sin listed is condemned in Scripture. In many lists of costly sins, pride is at or near the top. It was pride that led to Satan's expulsion from heaven. It was pride that led to the fall of mankind. Pride has been and still is one of the most deadly sins because pride robs us of our ability to see our need for God.

Read Proverbs 16:18. Where does pride lead?

_____

_____

_____

JOURNEY THROUGH GOD'S WORD

In the Bible, *hate* is used to describe a strong negative reaction generally directed toward an enemy. The term is used in reference to the relationships between people and the relationship between God and people.

Hatred between people is the result of jealousy and envy. It can lead to violence and even murder. Hatred was prohibited by Hebrew law, but that didn't make it disappear. Throughout Scripture, hatred is condemned while love for each other is encouraged. Hatred is a part of the old life (Galatians 5:19–21). Jesus encouraged love as a viable replacement for the tendency to hate.

There are some situations in which hatred is commanded. Believers are instructed to hate the things God

---

hates and the things that oppose God. However, believers are never instructed to hate people. Jesus said that His followers would have to hate their families in order to follow Him (Luke 14:26). This isn't the same as interpersonal animosity; it is the conscious establishment of priorities. *Hate* here means to love family less than you love Jesus. Believers also are instructed to hate their own lives in order to obtain eternal life (John 12:25).

Believers in Jesus Christ should expect to be hated by the world. Jesus suggested that believers rejoice when they experience hatred (Luke 6:22–23).

The Bible does describe situations in which God is viewed as hating something. God is holy and, therefore, is disturbed by sin. God hates idolatry (Deuteronomy 12:31) and hypocritical worship (Isaiah 1:14). God hates sin (Proverbs 8:13), but He loves the sinner. The Bible is clear that God's hatred is directed toward specific activities rather than toward individuals.

God's hatred is His moral reaction to sin—a reaction that He wants to cultivate in the lives of His people.[2]

The only way that we can cultivate God's character in our lives is to develop a strong relationship with Him. That takes time and commitment above what most people are willing to offer.

In our dealings with other people and ourselves, we must keep in mind that God loves us no matter what we do. However, we also must remember that, in spite of His love for us, God sometimes has divine hatred for some of our attitudes and actions. In this lesson, we'll take a look at some of the most destructive human tendencies.

RETHINK

What is one situation in which pride has been a problem for you?

_____

_____

_____

What are you doing to control your pride?

_____

_____

_____

We've heard it said that the entire human race is beset with "I" trouble. This is different from "eye" trouble. "Eye" trouble prevents us from seeing the world around us the way it should be seen. "I" trouble prevents us from seeing ourselves the way we should be seen.

Read Isaiah 14:13–14. What is the primary personal problem revealed in this statement?

_____

_____

_____

The temptation that has plagued humanity throughout all of history has been the desire to be like God. It was Adam and Eve's problem (Genesis 3:5), and it is our problem. However, there is a danger associated with this desire.

Read Proverbs 16:18. What is the ultimate danger associated with pride?

_____

_____

_____

REFLECT

Many parents teach their children to take pride in their school-work and their appearance. Some people take pride in their yards and their homes. Others value their cars, possessions, jobs, and education in prideful ways. Pride, like salt, can easily be overused. Let's take a look at three things pride does to us.

1. **Pride blinds us to our faults.**
   When we are full of pride, we are convinced that we are better or more important than we really are.

Read Luke 18:11. What is the attitude expressed in this verse?

_____

_____

_____

Read Luke 18:13. What is the attitude expressed in this verse?

_____

_____

_____

Which person described in these verses are you most like? Explain your answer.

_____

_____

_____

_____

Sometimes the faults we find in other people are the very faults we have in our own lives. If we criticize someone's rudeness, we need to be sure we aren't overlooking our own rudeness. It is easy to find faults in other people, but turning that evaluation on ourselves is something we resist.

What are the characteristics of others that you most criticize?

_____

_____

_____

_____

To what degree do you exhibit these same qualities?

_____

_____

_____

_____

_____

2. **Pride cuts us off from others.**

   Pride puts us above others and interferes with interpersonal relationships. No one likes prideful, arro-
   gant people. It is pride that is at the root of many
   social attitudes that have been part of our national
   history.

Maybe you can justify prejudice and racism in your own mind.
You can even justify these attitudes to family, friends, neighbors, and people you don't know. You can rationalize hatred for
others and join organizations to spread that hatred. But one
thing remains true—_you can never justify prejudice and racism
to God._

Read Revelation 5:9. Who was purchased for God by Jesus' blood? Was anyone excluded?

_____

_____

_____

_____

_____

No race or ethnic group is superior to any other race or ethnic group. Jesus Christ died for all people. If you harbor pride that puts you above other people, you are not living in the truth of God's Word.

3. **Pride cuts us off from God.**

   The Bible is rich with examples of people who serve as great examples of faith in action. It also has some stories of people who let their faith suffer as their humanity gained control of their lives.

Read 2 Chronicles 26:16. What was the downfall of King Uzziah?

_____

_____

_____

_____

Read Micah 6:8. What are the attitudes God requires of you?

_____

_____

_____

_____

Pride is sin; sin separates from God. Therefore, pride separates us from God. When you evaluate your relationship with Him, you might be surprised to discover the barrier that pride has erected in your life.

Does this mean pride is always wrong? No, it isn't—if properly understood. It's not wrong to take pride in a job well done, for example, or in the accomplishments of those we love—as long as we acknowledge that God gave us our abilities and He alone deserves the credit. Nor is it wrong to have a proper sense of self-esteem and self-confidence. The key is balance—avoiding both selfish, egocentric pride and unjustified self-loathing.

BILLY GRAHAM
The Journey

There is a second pair of enemies that cause problems for many believers—envy and greed. Envy and greed have been at the heart of the downfalls of corporations, politicians, and families. Adam and Eve were infected with envy and greed—they wanted to have what God had and to be like Him.

There aren't any biblical examples of greed and envy being anything other than destructive. Envy and greed rob people of peace and disrupt their relationships with God and the people around them. Here are a few of the effects of envy and greed.

Envy and greed are costly. When we focus all of our energies on getting something or being like someone else, we have lowered our eyes from an awareness of God. One of the most tragic examples of the price of greed is the story of Ananias and Sapphira.

Read Acts 5:1–11. Briefly summarize the story in the space below.

_____

_____

_____

_____

_____

What is the moral of the story?

_____

_____

_____

Envy and greed harm society. Maybe you remember a day when people left their doors unlocked and trusted their neighbors. Do you remember a time when there weren't security cameras and home alarm systems? All of these devices represent our efforts to protect our families and property against envy and greed.

People today invest their lives trying to scam others. The default in our culture is skepticism rather than trust.

Read James 4:1–2. What is the progression of envy and greed as described by James?

_____

_____

_____

Envy and greed harm us personally. Families are being torn apart by addictions to gambling. People take resources intended to meet the needs of their families and invest them in games of chance that they have little or no chance of winning. Marriage counselors point to financial trouble as the number-one cause of divorce.

Read 1 Timothy 6:10. What are some things you do because you love money?

_____

_____

_____

How is your love of money affecting your personal life?

_____

_____

_____

The love of money turns many people into workaholics and, as a result, their families pay the price. Children today are getting more and more time with paid caregivers and less and less time with their parents. Many times, both parents must work to make ends meet, but many parents sacrifice their family's health for the pursuit of bigger houses, nicer cars, and expensive clothing. Is the reward really worth the price?

REACT

Pride, greed, and envy are so common that many believers accept them as normal. Yet they are destructive in our lives and in our society. How can you avoid these dangers?

1. *Admit your problem and ask God to forgive you.*
   You know when you are prideful, greedy, and envious. Confess your sin to God so that it doesn't erect a barrier between you and Him.

Read 1 Peter 5:6. What can you do to make this verse a reality in your life?

_____

_____

_____

2. *Learn to walk in God's presence every day.*
   Pride, greed, and envy cannot be where God is because they are not a part of His character. The more you develop godly character, the more you will see your tendencies to have these damaging attitudes.

How will you develop God's character in your life?

_____

_____

_____

3. *Ask God to help you learn the secret of true contentment.*
   Rather than consider what you don't have in light of what other people have, consider what you have in light of what you deserve. We deserve to be eternally

separated from God. But God has given us the opportunity to be His children. Contentment is the mark of maturing faith.

> *Make thanksgiving a part of your daily life. Envy and greed starve on a steady diet of thanksgiving!*
> BILLY GRAHAM
> *The Journey*

Read 1 Thessalonians 5:18. Can this verse be a daily reality for you? Why or why not?

_____

_____

_____

4. *Learn to trust God in everything.*

God gives us what we need when we need it. God, however, doesn't give us what we want when we want it. God's blessings are His way of working through His children to affect the world around them. God's blessings are never intended to be hoarded. God blesses you so that you can show Him to the world.

Read Hebrews 13:5 and Philippians 4:11. How can you become more content in your life?

_____

_____

_____

What does God see when He looks at your heart? Does He see pride, greed, or envy? Does He see peace and contentment? What do you want Him to see?

_____

_____

_____

> *Recommit your whole life to Christ—including your innermost thoughts and desires. Then ask God to begin changing you from within by the power of His Spirit.*
> BILLY GRAHAM
> *The Journey*

What are three truths you learned in this study, and how will you apply each truth to your daily life?

1. _____

_____

_____

2. _____

_____

_____

3. _____

_____

_____

NOTES

CHAPTER 1

1. Bob Kelly, *Worth Repeating*, 2003. Grand Rapids, MI: Kregel Publications, 379.
2. *Holman Illustrated Bible Dictionary*, 2003. Nashville, TN: B&H, 1163.

CHAPTER 2

1. Bob Kelly, *Worth Repeating*, 314.
2. *Holman Illustrated Bible Dictionary*, 622.

CHAPTER 3

1. Bob Kelly, *Worth Repeating*, 285.
2. *Holman Illustrated Bible Dictionary*, 1568–1569.

CHAPTER 4

1. Bob Kelly, *Worth Repeating*, 339.
2. *Holman Illustrated Bible Dictionary*, 1292–1293.

CHAPTER 5

1. Bob Kelly, *Worth Repeating*, 307.
2. *Holman Illustrated Bible Dictionary*, 731–732.

Chapter 6

1. Bob Kelly, *Worth Repeating*, 314.
2. *Holman Illustrated Bible Dictionary*, 723.

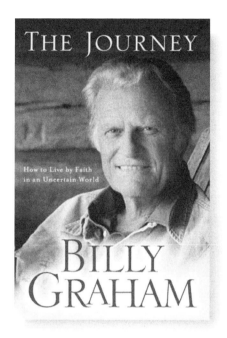

Billy Graham is respected and loved around the world.
The Journey is his magnum opus, the culmination of a
lifetime of experience and ministry. With insight that comes
only from a life spent with God, this book is filled with
wisdom, encouragement, hope, and inspiration for anyone
who wants to live a happier, more fulfilling life.

978-0-8499-1887-2 (PB)

STUDY GUIDE NOTES

STUDY GUIDE NOTES

STUDY GUIDE NOTES